Contents

Words in **bold** are
in the glossary.

What is clay?

Clay is a **natural material**. It is useful because it is easy to make into different shapes.

There are two kinds of clay - china clay and ball clay. China clay is white and smooth. We use it for making **crockery**, such as teapots, mugs and eggcups.

Things made from china clay are called pottery.

How we **USE** materials

Clay

Rita Storey

W
FRANKLIN WATTS
LONDON•SYDNEY

First published in 2006 by
Franklin Watts
338 Euston Road
London NW1 3BH

Franklin Watts Australia
Hachette Children's Books
Level 17/207 Kent Street
Sydney NSW 2000

Art director: Jonathan Hair
Series designed and created for Franklin Watts by Painted Fish Ltd.
Designer: Rita Storey
Editor: Fiona Corbridge

Picture credits:
Corbis/Andrew Brown p. 8, Corbis/Jacqui Hurst p. 11 (top), Corbis/David Samuel
Robbins p. 10; istockphoto.com p. 7 (top and bottom), p. 9 (top and middle), p. 11
(bottom), p. 12, p. 13, p. 15 (bottom), p. 16, p. 17 (top), p. 18, p. 19, p. 21, p. 23, p.
24, p. 25 (top and middle), p. 26 (bottom), p. 27; Tudor Photography p. 3, p. 5, p. 6,
p. 7 (middle), p. 9 (bottom), p. 10 (bottom). p. 14, p. 15 (top), p. 17 (bottom), p. 20,
p. 22, p. 25 (bottom), p. 26 (top).

Cover images: Tudor Photography, Banbury

ISBN-10: 0 7496 6460 6
ISBN-13: 978 0 7496 6460 2
Dewey classification: 666'.42

A CIP catalogue record for this book is available from the British Library.

Printed in China

We make pottery **ornaments**, such as this bowl, to decorate our homes. Some ornaments are fun to own, like this piggy bank.

Clay keywords
Ceramics
China clay
Pottery
Ball clay

Ball clay is rough. It is **hard-wearing**, so it is used to make bricks and building materials.

Things made from china clay or ball clay are called **ceramics**.

Where does clay come from?

Clay is a kind of earth.
It is soft when it is wet,
and it is easy to shape.

To get clay, we dig **pits** in the ground. Water jets are used to wash the clay out of soil and rock. The clay is cleaned and then it is ready to use.

To make things from clay, we shape it while it is soft, wet and sticky.

When clay dries, it becomes hard. To make it even harder, we **fire** it (bake it) in a special oven called a **kiln**. Once clay has been fired, it will not become soft again.

Clay keywords
Shape
Fire
Brittle
Kiln

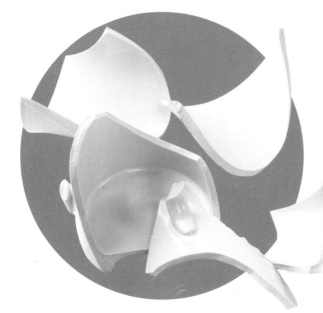

Clay that has been fired is hard but it is also **brittle**. It will chip or break if you drop it.

Shaping clay

Clay is easy to shape with our hands. This makes it a good material for artists to use.

Artists called sculptors use clay to make models of people and animals.

Potters make useful things out of clay, such as bowls and vases.

Sometimes potters use flat slabs of clay to make things. They can also roll out the clay into a long rope and coil it up to make a pot.

Pots can also be shaped on a wheel that spins round. This is called **throwing.**

Clay keywords
Sculptor
Potter
Throwing

Using a mould

We can shape clay in a **mould** to make different objects for our homes.

- We can make clay shapes by mixing clay with water and pouring the liquid into a mould. When the clay dries, it is the shape of the mould. Some baths are made like this.

If you use a mould you can make the same shape again and again.

There are many washbasins the same shape as this one.

Wall tiles are thin, flat pieces of clay. They are shaped by pressing them into a mould.

Clay keywords

Mould
Bath
Washbasin
Tiles

Clay in the kitchen

Clay is good for making jars, dishes, cups and plates.

When clay has been fired, it is hard but it will still soak up water. To make it **waterproof**, we put a coating called a **glaze** on it.

Clay that has been glazed can be used to hold food and drink, such as this bowl and mug. They are easy to wash afterwards.

● Some pottery is cheap to make but it cracks easily. This type of pottery is called **earthenware**. We use it for everyday things such as these storage jars.

Clay keywords

Waterproof
Glaze
Earthenware
Stoneware

We use some clay dishes for cooking in the oven. They are made of strong pottery called **stoneware**. It will not crack when it is heated.

Porcelain

Porcelain is fine pottery, which is thin enough to let light shine through it. It is pure white when it is fired.

We can make porcelain into very small shapes like these ornaments.

Porcelain ornaments are often painted by hand. This means that each piece is slightly different.

Clay keywords
Porcelain
Thin
Bone china

Bone china is a strong porcelain. It is used to make **tea sets** and **dinner services**.

Clay for building

When clay is fired it goes hard. This makes it useful for building.

- We use clay to make bricks for houses. Bricks are usually shaped in a mould.

Clay pipes like these are used to take dirty water and sewage away from your home.

If we mix clay with **limestone**, it makes **cement**. Cement is used to make **mortar**. We stick bricks together with mortar.

When we mix cement with sand, gravel and water, it makes **concrete**. Concrete is a good material for building with because it is strong and hard.

Clay keywords
Bricks
Cement
Concrete
Mortar

Clay outdoors

Clay is not harmed by sun and rain, so it can be used to make things that are left outside.

Flowerpots are sometimes made of an orangey-red ball clay called **terracotta**. This kind of clay is fired but not glazed.

Floor and roof tiles are sometimes made of terracotta. The colour of terracotta looks attractive.

Clay keywords

Terracotta

Tiles that have been glazed are waterproof. The tiles on this swimming pool stop the water leaking out.

Clay at school

Many things you use at school are made with clay.

- Some paper is coated with china clay to give it a smooth, shiny surface. The clay also makes it very white and bright. We write and print on this kind of paper.

Modelling clay is a good material for making pots and models because it is easy to shape.

The plastics used to make the outside of computers have china clay in them to make them strong.

Crayons sometimes have china clay in them to make them smooth to use.

Other uses of clay

Here are some more uses of clay that you may not have thought of.

Some **tennis courts** are made from clay. The ball bounces high on a clay court because the clay is hard.

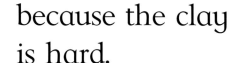

Dentists can fix a type of porcelain to teeth to make them look better. It is smooth, white and very strong.

● Some things made of rubber, such as this tyre, have clay in them to make them last longer.

● This paste is used to fill cracks in walls. It has china clay in it to make it thick.

Clay keywords

Hard
White
Strong

Clay powder

Factories put clay powder into many different things when they make them.

- Some toothpastes have china clay in them. The clay helps to make the toothpaste **flow** out of the tube.

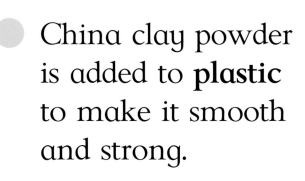

China clay powder is added to **plastic** to make it smooth and strong.

Paint has china clay in it to make it thick and smooth.

Clay powder is put into bars of soap to help them keep their shape. It is safe to use on our skin.

Washing powder has clay in it to stop it sticking together in a big lump.

Clay keywords

Flow
Smooth
Thick

Glossary

Bone china Porcelain with other things added to make it very strong.

Brittle A material that is hard but breaks easily when it is dropped.

Cement A fine powder of limestone and clay. It is used to make mortar and concrete.

Ceramics Objects made from clay.

Concrete A mixture of cement, water, sand and small stones. It is used to build with.

Crockery Eating and serving dishes made of earthenware.

Dinner services Sets of pottery or porcelain items used for serving and eating dinner.

Earthenware A type of china clay used for everyday things such as jars.

Fire To bake in a kiln.

Flow Move freely.

Glaze A smooth, shiny coating.

Hard-wearing To last a long time without breaking or rotting.

Kiln A special oven used for baking clay pots.

Limestone A white rock. Powdered limestone is used to make cement.

Modelling clay A type of clay used to make models.

Mortar A mixture of cement, sand and water that is used to stick bricks or stones together. It hardens when it is dry.

Mould A shape that clay is poured into to make an object in that shape.

Natural material Comes from the Earth, plants or animals.

Ornaments Objects that look attractive.

Pits Holes in the ground.

Plastic A material that is made in factories.

Porcelain Smooth white pottery.

Stoneware A strong kind of china clay, which is used for dishes that will be put in an oven.

Tea sets All the pieces of pottery or porcelain that you need to have tea.

Tennis courts Marked-out areas where people play tennis.

Terracotta A orangey-red clay used to make flowerpots and roof tiles.

Throwing Making pots on a wheel that spins round.

Waterproof Does not let water pass through.

Index